CAT CHAT

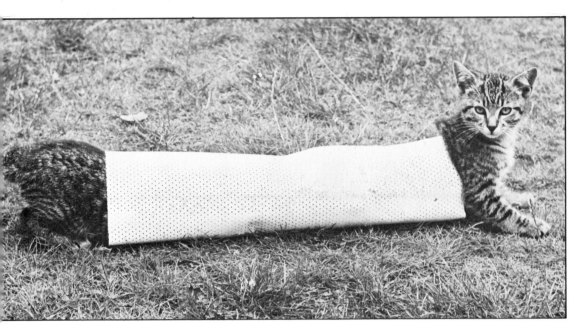

Edited by
PETER FINCHAM

Captions by Clive Anderson, Peter Fincham,
John Lloyd, Rory McGrath and Laurie Rowley

Picture research by Jane Ross

ARROW

Arrow Books Limited
20 Vauxhall Bridge Road, London SW1V 2SA

An imprint of Random Century Group

London Melbourne Sydney Auckland Johannesburg
and agencies throughout the world

First published by Arrow Books 1988
      12 14 15 13 11

Printed in England by Clays Ltd, St Ives plc

ISBN 0 09 964040 6

The authors and publishers gratefully acknowledge the following picture libraries
for permission to reproduce material:

Barnaby's Picture Library – front cover photograph, 1, 14, 15, 19, 32, 39, 43, 44, 57;
BBC Hulton Picture Library – 2, 3, 4, 5, 6, 9, 11, 29, 46, 50, 52, 61, 62; The Keystone
Collection – 8, 10, 13, 16, 33, 36 (i and ii), 45, 47, 53, 55, 56, 60, 63; Kobal Collection –
26, 30; Popperfoto – title page, 12, 17, 20, 24/25, 27, 28, 31, 34, 37, 38 (ii), 41, 48, 49, 51,
58, 64; S & G Press Agency – 40; Syndication International – 7, 18, 21, 22, 23, 35, 38
(i), 42, 54, 59.

1

3

5

23

29

41

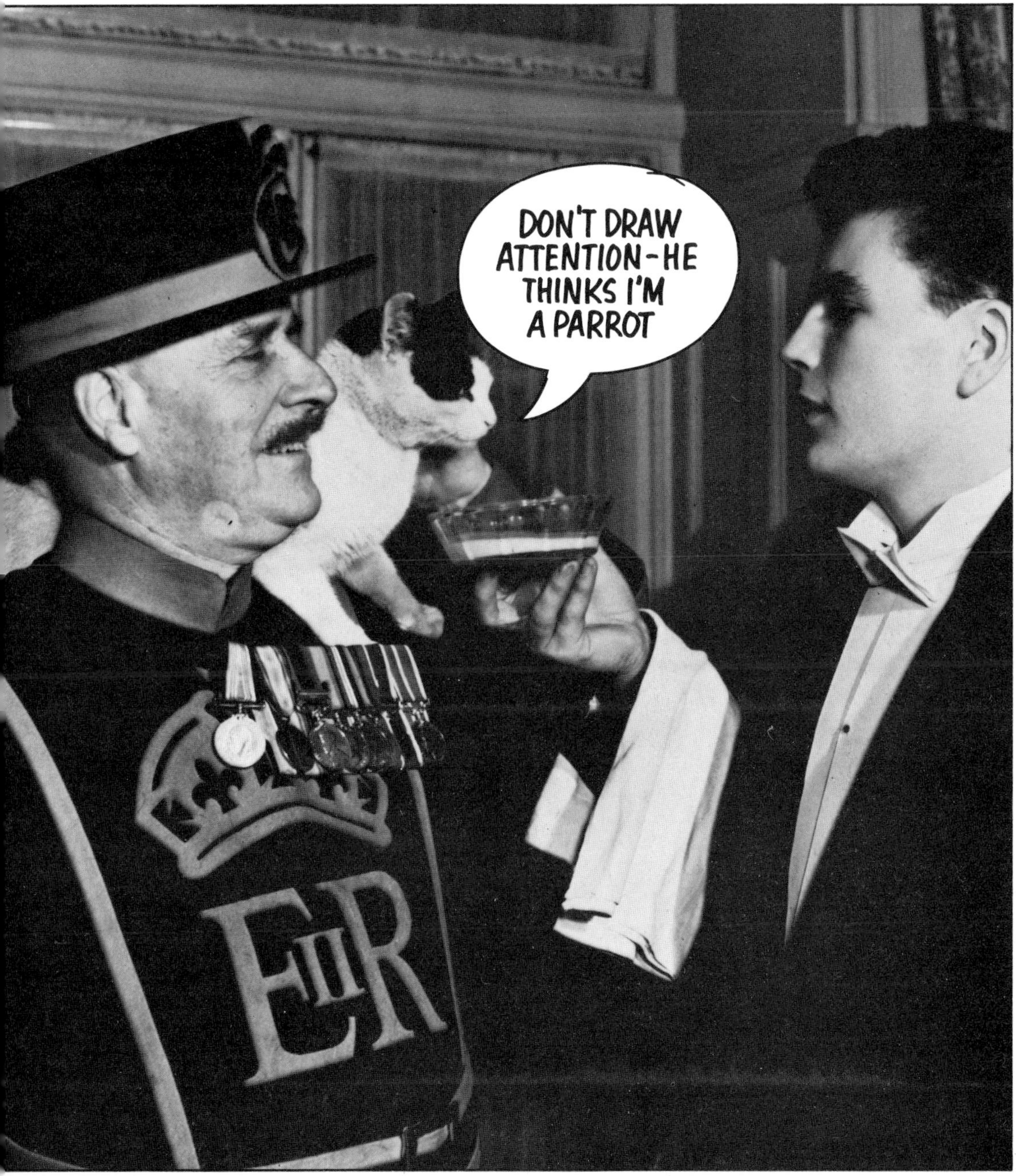
DON'T DRAW ATTENTION-HE THINKS I'M A PARROT
EIIR